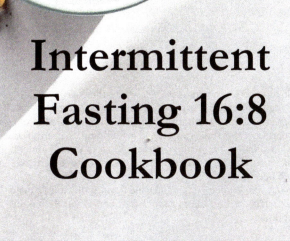

Intermittent Fasting 16:8 Cookbook

Guaranteed No Stress I.F. Recipes The Whole Family Will Love!

Yasmin Bateman

DIETABLE PRESS

© Copyright 2021. All rights reserved.

The following Book is reproduced below with the goal of providing information that is as accurate and reliable as possible. Regardless, purchasing this Book can be seen as consent to the fact that both the publisher and the author of this book are in no way experts on the topics discussed within and that any recommendations or suggestions that are made herein are for entertainment purposes only. Professionals should be consulted as needed prior to undertaking any of the action endorsed herein.

This declaration is deemed fair and valid by both the American Bar Association and the Committee of Publishers Association and is legally binding throughout the United States.

Furthermore, the transmission, duplication, or reproduction of any of the following work including specific information will be considered an illegal act irrespective of if it is done electronically or in print. This extends to creating a secondary or tertiary copy of the work or a recorded copy and is only allowed with the express written consent from the Publisher. All additional right reserved.

The information in the following pages is broadly considered a truthful and accurate account of facts and as such, any inattention, use, or misuse of the information in question by the reader will render any resulting actions solely under their purview. There are no scenarios in which the publisher or the original author of this work can be in any fashion deemed liable for any hardship or damages that may befall them after undertaking information described herein.

Additionally, the information in the following pages is intended only for informational purposes and should thus be thought of as universal. As befitting its nature, it is presented without assurance regarding its prolonged validity or interim quality. Trademarks that are mentioned are done without written consent and can in no way be considered an endorsement from the trademark holder.

CONTENTS

Lean and Green Smoothie 6
Medifast Patties 7
Green Colada Smoothie 9
Green Apple Smoothie 10
Spinach Smoothie 11
Kale and Cheese Muffins 12
Matcha Avocado Smoothie 14
Egg Cups 15
Sweet Potato Rounds 17
Zucchini Bites 19
Cauliflower Bites 21
Pancetta Wrapped Prunes 23
Turkey Lettuce Wraps 25
Bell Pepper Bites 27
Avocado Shrimp Cucumber 29
Queso Dip 31
Peanut Butter Cookies 33
Goat Cheese Crostini 35
Buffalo Cauliflower 36
Peanut Butter Brownie 38
Chocolate Cherry Cookie 39
Stuffed pears with almonds 40
Peanut Butter Cups 42
Medifast Rolls 43
Apple Crisp 45
Cherry Dessert 47
Vanilla Pudding 48
Banana Cookies 50

Sweet Potato Cheesecake 51
Cauliflower Breakfast Casserole 53
Quinoa Pudding 55
Cranberry Sweet Potato Muffins 56
Quinoa Bars 58
Buckwheat Crepes 60
Oatmeal Pancakes 62
Blueberry Muffins 64
Berry Quinoa 66
Celery Salad 68
Taco Salad 69
Yogurt Trail Mix Bars 70
Curried Tuna Salad 71
Tuna Quinoa Cakes 72
Taco Cups 74
Caprese Spaghetti Squash Nests 76
Fire Cracker Shrimp 78
Crispy Zucchini Chips 79
Baked Kale Chips 80
Chia Seed Pudding 81
Grilled Buffalo Shrimp 82
Strawberry Ice Cream 83
Strawberry Yogurt 84
Banana Pops 85
Strawberry Cheesecake 87
Coffee Cake Muffins 89
Peanut Butter Balls 90
Brownie in a Tray 91
Dark Chocolate Mousse 93

Banana Pudding 94
Garlic Chicken with Zoodles 96
Chicken Zucchini Boats 98
Medifast Chicken Fry 100
Tuscan Chicken 101
Chicken Taco Soup 103
Chicken Chili 104
Lean Green Chicken Soup 106
Avocado Chicken Salad 108
Chicken Pesto Pasta 109
Sesame Chicken Fry 111
Teriyaki Chicken Broccoli 114

Lean and Green Smoothie

Preparation Time: 5 minutes.

Cooking Time: 0 minutes.

Servings: 2

Ingredients:

- 2 ½ cups kale leaves, stemmed
- 1 cup pineapple, cubed
- ¾ cup apple juice, chilled
- ½ cup seedless green grapes, frozen
- ½ cup Granny Smith apple, chopped
- 1 cup green grapes, halved

Directions:

1. Blend kale with grapes with apple and pineapple in a blender.
2. Serve with halved grapes.
3. Enjoy.

How to serve: Enjoy this smoothie with breakfast muffins.

Optional: Add some strawberries to the smoothie.

Per Serving:

Calories 84 | Fat 7.9g |Sodium 704mg | Carbs 19g | Fiber 2g | Sugar 14g | Protein 1g

Medifast Patties

Preparation Time: 10 minutes.
Cooking Time: 20 minutes.
Servings: 4
Ingredients:

- 1 3/4 lbs. Dungeness crab meat
- 1 tablespoon red bell pepper, diced
- 1 tablespoon green bell pepper, diced
- 1 tablespoon parsley leaves, chopped
- 1 ½ tablespoon heavy mayonnaise
- 2 eggs 3 teaspoons baking powder
- 1 teaspoon Worcestershire sauce
- 1 teaspoon Old Bay seasoning
- 10 cooking spray

Directions:

1. Mix crab meat with bell peppers, parsley, mayonnaise, baking powder, Worcestershire sauce and old bay seasoning in a bowl.
2. Make small patties out of this mixture.
3. Set a skillet, greased with cooking spray, over medium heat.
4. Sear the patties for 5 minutes per side.
5. Enjoy.

How to serve: Serve these patties with toasted bread slices.
Optional: Add chopped carrots and broccoli to the cakes.

Per Serving:

Calories 214 | Fat 5.1g | Sodium 231mg | Carbs 31g | Fiber 5g | Sugar 2.1g | Protein 17g

Green Colada Smoothie

Preparation Time: 5 minutes.
Cooking Time: 0 minutes.
Servings: 2
Ingredients:

- 1 cup Greek yogurt
- 1 cup frozen pineapple
- 1 cup baby spinach
- ½ cup lite coconut milk
- ½ teaspoon vanilla extract
- Coconut flakes for garnish

Directions:

1. Blend yogurt with pineapple, spinach, coconut milk, and vanilla in a blender until smooth.
2. Garnish with coconut flakes and serve.

How to serve: Enjoy this smoothie with breakfast muffins.
Optional: Add some strawberries to the smoothie.
Per Serving:
Calories 325 | Fat 9g |Sodium 118mg | Carbs 35.4g | Fiber 2.9g | Sugar 15g | Protein 26.5g

Green Apple Smoothie

Preparation Time: 5 minutes.

Cooking Time: 0 minutes.

Servings: 2

Ingredients:

- 2 ripe bananas
- 1 ripe pear, peeled, chopped
- 2 cups kale leaves, chopped
- ½ cup of orange juice
- ½ cup of cold water
- 12 ice cubes
- 1 tablespoon ground flaxseed

Directions:

1. Blend bananas with pear, kale leaves, orange juice, cold water, ice cubes and flaxseed in a blender.
2. Serve.

How to serve: Serve this smoothie with morning muffins.

Optional: Add some strawberries to the smoothie.

Per Serving:

Calories 213 | Fat 2.5g | Sodium 15.6mg | Carbs 49.5g | Fiber 7.6g | Sugar 28g | Protein 3.5g

Spinach Smoothie

Preparation Time: 5 minutes.

Cooking Time: 0 minutes.

Servings: 2

Ingredients:

- 1 cup fresh spinach
- 1 banana
- ½ green apple
- 4 hulled strawberries
- 4 (1 inch) pieces frozen mango
- ⅓ cup whole milk
- 1 scoop vanilla protein powder
- 1 teaspoon honey

Directions:

1. Blend spinach with banana with the green apple with strawberries, mango, milk, protein powder and honey in a blender.
2. Serve.

How to serve: Enjoy this smoothie with breakfast muffins.

Optional: Add some blueberries to the smoothie.

Per Serving:

Calories 312 | Fat 25g | Sodium 132mg | Carbs 44g | Fiber 3.9g | Sugar 3g | Protein 18.9g

Kale and Cheese Muffins

Preparation Time: 10 minutes.

Cooking Time: 25 minutes.

Servings: 9

Ingredients:

- 9 large eggs
- 1 cup liquid egg whites
- 3/4 cup plain Greek yogurt
- 2 ounces goat cheese crumbled
- 1/2 teaspoon salt
- 10 ounces kale
- 2 cups cherry tomatoes
- cooking spray

Directions:

1. At 375 degrees F, preheat your oven.
2. Beat eggs with goat cheese, yogurt, and egg whites in a bowl.
3. Stir in cherry tomatoes and kale, then divide this mixture into a muffin tray.
4. Bake the muffin cups for 25 minutes in the preheated oven.
5. Enjoy.

How to serve: Serve these muffins with a green smoothie.

Optional: Add chopped nuts to the batter.

Per Serving:

Calories 290 | Fat 15g |Sodium 595mg | Carbs 11g | Fiber 3g | Sugar 12g | Protein 29g

Matcha Avocado Smoothie

Preparation Time: 5 minutes.

Cooking Time: 0 minutes.

Servings: 2

Ingredients:

- 1/2 avocado, peeled and cubed
- 1/3 cucumber
- 2 cups spinach
- 6 ounces coconut milk
- 6 ounces almond milk
- 1 teaspoon matcha powder
- 1/2 lime juice
- 1/2 scoop vanilla protein powder
- 1/2 teaspoon chia seeds

Directions:

1. Blend avocado flesh with cucumber and the rest of the ingredients in a blender until smooth.
2. Serve.

How to serve: Enjoy this smoothie with breakfast muffins.

Optional: Add some strawberries to the smoothie.

Per Serving:

Calories 297 | Fat 15g | Sodium 202mg | Carbs 58.5g | Fiber 4g | Sugar 1g | Protein 7.3g

Egg Cups

Preparation Time: 10 minutes.
Cooking Time: 13 minutes.
Servings: 4
Ingredients:

- 4 eggs
- 8 egg whites
- ¼ c chopped green chilies
- 1 bunch green onions chopped
- 12 pieces of Canadian bacon
- 1 cup ripped spinach
- 1/8 teaspoons salt
- ½ teaspoons black pepper

Directions:

1. Beat eggs with egg whites, green chilies, green onions, spinach, black pepper and salt in a bowl.
2. Place a bacon slice in each muffin cup of a muffin tray and press it.
3. Divide the egg mixture into the bacon cup.
4. Bake for 13 minutes in the oven at 350 degrees F.
5. Serve warm.

How to serve: Serve these cups with a green smoothie.
Optional: Add sautéed ground chicken to the egg filling.

Per Serving:

Calories 163 | Fat 6.5g |Sodium 548mg | Carbs 3.4g | Fiber 2g | Sugar 1g | Protein 22g

Sweet Potato Rounds

Preparation Time: 15 minutes.
Cooking Time: 22 minutes.
Servings: 6
Ingredients:

- 2 lbs. sweet potatoes
- 1 ½ tablespoons olive oil
- 1 teaspoon garlic powder
- 1 teaspoon chili powder
- 1 teaspoon salt
- Hot sauce
- Monterrey Jack and cheddar cheese, shredded
- 3 green onions
- Sour cream

Directions:

1. At 450 degrees F, preheat your oven.
2. Slice the sweet potatoes into ¼ inch thick slices.
3. Toss the slices with 1 teaspoon salt, 1 teaspoon chili powder, 1 teaspoon garlic powder and 1 ½ tablespoon olive oil in a large bowl.
4. Spread these slices in a baking sheet, lined with parchment paper.
5. Bake the sweet potato slices for 10 minutes, flip and bake again for 10 minutes.

6. Top each potato slice with green onions, a dot of hot sauce, and shredded cheese.
7. Bake the potatoes for 2 minutes until the cheese is melted.
8. Garnish with sour cream and serve warm.

How to serve: Serve these rounds with tomato ketchup or cheese dip.

Optional: Drizzle cinnamon ground on top.

Per Serving:

Calories 148 | Fat 22g |Sodium 350mg | Carbs 32.2g | Fiber 0.7g | Sugar 1g | Protein 4.3g

Zucchini Bites

Preparation Time: 15 minutes.

Cooking Time: 10 minutes.

Servings: 6

Ingredients:

- 2 large zucchinis
- ½ cup pizza sauce
- 1 teaspoon oregano
- 2 cups mozzarella cheese
- ¼ cup parmesan cheese

Directions:

1. At 450 degrees F, preheat your oven. Layer a baking sheet with a foil sheet.
2. Cut the zucchini into ¼ inch thick slice and place them on the baking sheet.
3. Top each slice with pizza sauce, oregano, and cheese.
4. Bake the zucchini slices for 5-10 minutes until the cheese is melted.
5. Serve warm.

How to serve: Serve the bites with cheese or yogurt dip.

Optional: Drizzle black pepper ground on top before baking.

Per Serving:

Calories 145 | Fat 9g | Sodium 48mg | Carbs 4g | Fiber 1g | Sugar 2g | Protein 10g

Cauliflower Bites

Preparation Time: 15 minutes.
Cooking Time: 20 minutes.
Servings: 8
Ingredients:

- 8 cups cauliflower florets
- 2 tablespoons olive oil
- ¼ teaspoon kosher salt
- 2 tablespoons hot sauce
- 1-2 tablespoons Sriracha
- 1 tablespoon butter, melted
- 1 tablespoon lemon juice

Directions:

1. At 450 degrees F, preheat your oven.
2. Layer a rimmed baking sheet with cooking spray.
3. Toss cauliflower with salt and oil in a large bowl and spread evenly on the baking sheet.
4. Roast the cauliflower florets for 15 minutes in the preheated oven.
5. Mix hot sauce, lemon juice, butter and sriracha in a large bowl.
6. Toss in cauliflower and mix well to coat.
7. Return the cauliflower to the baking sheet and bake for 5 minutes.
8. Serve warm.

How to serve: Serve the cauliflower bites with tomato sauce.

Optional: Coat the cauliflower with breadcrumbs before cooking.

Per Serving:

Calories 104 | Fat 3g |Sodium 216mg | Carbs 17g | Fiber 3g | Sugar 4g | Protein 1g

Pancetta Wrapped Prunes

Preparation Time: 15 minutes.
Cooking Time: 11 minutes.
Servings: 8
Ingredients:

- 16 prunes, pitted
- 150g of Gorgonzola
- 16 pancetta slices
- 3 tablespoons vegetable oil
- 3 tablespoons of walnuts
- 1 handful of celery leaves
- Black pepper, to taste

Directions:

1. Add prunes with water to a cooking pot, cover and boil for 5 minutes then drain.
2. Pat dry the prunes, and remove their pits.
3. Dice the gorgonzola into 16 cubes and insert one cube into each pitted prune.
4. Wrap each prune with a pancetta slice and insert a toothpick to secure it.
5. Set a pan with cooking oil over medium heat and sear the wrapped prunes for 2-3 minutes per side.
6. Garnish with walnuts, black pepper and celery leaves.
7. Enjoy.

How to serve: Serve the rolls with mayonnaise dip.

Optional: Drizzle shredded coconut on top before serving.

Per Serving:

Calories 180 | Fat 9g | Sodium 318mg | Carbs 19g | Fiber 5g | Sugar 3g | Protein 7g

Turkey Lettuce Wraps

Preparation Time: 15 minutes.
Cooking Time: 8 minutes.
Servings: 6
Ingredients:

- 1 lb. lean ground turkey
- 1 tablespoon vegetable oil
- 1 small onion, diced
- 2 garlic cloves, minced
- 1 teaspoon ginger, grated
- 1 bell pepper, diced
- 1 tablespoon soy sauce
- 2 tablespoons Hoisin
- 1 teaspoon sesame oil
- 2 teaspoons rice vinegar
- 2 green onions, minced
- Salt, to taste
- Black pepper, to taste
- Fresh lettuce leaves

Directions:

1. Sauté onion with ginger, garlic and cooking oil in a large pan until soft.
2. Stir in turkey ground and sauté for 3 minutes.
3. Add rice vinegar, sesame oil, hoisin and soy sauce then mix well.

4. Stir in green onion and bell peppers then sauté for 5 minutes.
5. Adjust seasoning with black pepper and salt.
6. Divide this filling into the lettuce leaves.
7. Serve.

How to serve: Serve the wraps with cream cheese dip on the side.

Optional: Toss turkey meat with shredded parmesan before cooking.

Per Serving:

Calories 173 | Fat 8g |Sodium 146mg | Carbs 18g | Fiber 5g | Sugar 1g | Protein 7g

Bell Pepper Bites

Preparation Time: 15 minutes.

Cooking Time: 4 minutes.

Servings: 9

Ingredients:

- 1 medium green bell pepper
- 1 medium red bell pepper
- 1/4 cup almonds, sliced
- 4 ounces low-fat cream cheese
- 1 teaspoon lemon pepper seasoning blend
- 1 teaspoon lemon juice

Directions:

1. Slice the peppers in half, lengthwise.
2. Destem and deseed the peppers and cut each half into 6 more pieces.
3. Roast almonds in a skillet for 4 minutes then grind in a food processor.
4. Mix cream cheese with lemon juice and lemon pepper in a mixing bowl for 2 minutes.
5. Stir in the almond ground and mix for 10 seconds.
6. Add this filling to the piping bag and pipe this mixture into the bell pepper piece.
7. Serve.

How to serve: Serve the peppers with chilli sauce or mayo dip.

Optional: Add shredded cheese to the filling.

Per Serving:

Calories 140 | Fat 5g |Sodium 244mg | Carbs 16g | Fiber 1g | Sugar 1g | Protein 17g

Avocado Shrimp Cucumber

Preparation Time: 15 minutes.
Cooking Time: 6 minutes.
Servings: 4
Ingredients:

- 1 cucumber, sliced into 1/2-inch slices
- 2 large avocados, halved and pitted
- Salt and black pepper to taste
- 2 teaspoons lemon juice

Marinade:

- 2 lbs. shrimp, peeled and deveined
- 2 garlic cloves, minced
- 1 1/2 teaspoon salt
- 1/2 teaspoon cayenne pepper
- 1 teaspoon paprika
- 3 tablespoons olive oil
- 1 tablespoon lemon juice

Directions:

1. Mix shrimp with garlic, salt, cayenne pepper, paprika, olive oil and lemon juice.
2. Cover and leave this marinade for 30 minutes.
3. Mash avocado with black pepper and salt in a bowl.
4. At medium-high heat, preheat your grill.
5. Grill the shrimp in the grill for 3 minutes per side.

6. Set the cucumber slices on the serving platter.
7. Top these slices with avocado mash and place a grilled shrimp on top.
8. Enjoy.

How to serve: Serve the bites with spinach or cream cheese dip.

Optional: Add shredded parmesan on top.

Per Serving:
Calories 82 | Fat 4g |Sodium 232mg | Carbs 7g | Fiber 1g | Sugar 0g | Protein 4g

Queso Dip

Preparation Time: 15 minutes.
Cooking Time: 12 minutes.
Servings: 8
Ingredients:

- 1 lb. lean ground turkey
- 1 small onion diced
- 1 package. taco seasoning
- 2 tablespoons butter
- 2 ½ tablespoons flour
- 1 ½ cup milk
- 1/2 teaspoon salt
- 1/8 teaspoons black pepper
- 4 ounces sharp cheddar shredded
- 4 ounces can jalapeños drained, diced

Directions:

1. Sauté turkey with onion in a large skillet until golden.
2. Add taco seasoning then mix well.
3. Sauté flour with butter in another pan for 2 minutes.
4. Remove it from the heat, pour in the milk and mix well until lump-free.
5. Add cheddar cheese, black pepper and salt then mix well until melted.

6. Stir in turkey meat mixture and diced jalapenos.
7. Serve warm.

How to serve: Serve the dip with zucchini fries.

Optional: Add olive slices or tomato salad on top.

Per Serving:

Calories 229 | Fat 5g |Sodium 510mg | Carbs 37g | Fiber 5g | Sugar 4g | Protein 11g

Peanut Butter Cookies

Preparation Time: 15 minutes.

Cooking Time: 12 minutes.

Servings: 4

Ingredients:

- 4 sachets optavia silky peanut butter shake
- 1/4 teaspoon baking powder
- 1/4 cup unsweetened almond milk
- 1 tablespoon butter, melted
- 1/4 teaspoon vanilla extract
- 1/8 teaspoon salt

Directions:

1. At 350 degrees F, preheat your oven.
2. Mix baking powder with peanut butter fueling in a bowl.
3. Stir in vanilla extract, melted butter, and almond milk, then mix until smooth.
4. Divide the dough into 8 cookies and place in a baking sheet, lined with parchment paper.
5. Flatten the cookies and bake for 12 minutes in the preheated oven.
6. Allow the cookies to cool and serve.

How to serve: Serve the cookies with pure maple or apple sauce.

Optional: Drizzle maple syrup on top before serving.

Per Serving:

Calories 201 | Fat 7g | Sodium 269mg | Carbs 35g | Fiber 4g | Sugar 12g | Protein 6g

Goat Cheese Crostini

Preparation Time: 15 minutes.

Cooking Time: 10 minutes.

Servings: 2

Ingredients:

- 1 baguette
- 4-ounce goat cheese
- Honey
- Fresh mint, chopped
- Ground black pepper

Directions:

1. At 350 degrees F, preheat your oven.
2. Cut the baguette into thin slices, diagonally.
3. Place the baguette slices in a baking sheet and bake for 10 minutes.
4. Divide goat cheese, honey, herbs, and black pepper on top of the bread slices.
5. Enjoy.

How to serve: Serve the crostini with chilli garlic sauce.

Optional: Add sliced olives to the topping.

Per Serving:

Calories 348 | Fat 12g | Sodium 710mg | Carbs 44g | Fiber 5g | Sugar 3g | Protein 11g

Buffalo Cauliflower

Preparation Time: 15 minutes.

Cooking Time: 36 minutes.

Servings: 4

Ingredients:

Buffalo cauliflower

- 1 head cauliflower
- 2 tablespoons olive oil
- ½ teaspoon kosher salt

Buffalo sauce

- 2 tablespoons unsalted butter
- 1 garlic clove
- ¼ cup Frank's hot sauce

Blue cheese sauce

- 1 cup plain yogurt
- ½ cup blue cheese crumbles
- 1/4 teaspoon salt
- 1 teaspoon garlic powder
- Fresh ground black pepper
- Celery, to serve

Directions:

1. At 450 degrees F, preheat your oven.
2. Cut the cauliflower head into small florets and toss them with salt and olive oil on a baking sheet.

3. Bake the cauliflower for 35 minutes in the preheated oven.
4. For buffalo sauce, sauté garlic with butter in a saucepan for 30 seconds.
5. Stir in hot sauce and sauté for 30 seconds.
6. Toss in the cauliflower florets and mix well with the sauce.
7. For cheese dip, blend all its ingredients in a blender.
8. Serve the cauliflower with cream cheese dip.
9. Enjoy.

How to serve: Serve the florets with tomato ketchup.

Optional: Coat the cauliflower in breadcrumbs before cooking.

Per Serving:

Calories 175 | Fat 16g | Sodium 255mg | Carbs 31g | Fiber 1.2g | Sugar 5g | Protein 4.1g

Peanut Butter Brownie

Preparation Time: 15 minutes.
Cooking Time: 1 minute.
Servings: 4
Ingredients:

- 3 tablespoons peanut butter powder
- 3 tablespoons water
- 6 packets optavia double chocolate brownie fueling
- 1 cup of water

Directions:

1. Mix peanut butter powder with water and chocolate brownie in a bowl.
2. Divide this batter on a baking sheet lined with parchment paper into small mounds.
3. Cover and freeze for 40 minutes.
4. Serve.

How to serve: Serve the brownies with chocolate dip.
Optional: Dip the brownies in white chocolate syrup.
Per Serving:
Calories 361 | Fat 10g | Sodium 218mg | Carbs 56g | Fiber 10g | Sugar 30g | Protein 14g

Chocolate Cherry Cookie

Preparation Time: 15 minutes.

Cooking Time: 12 minutes.

Servings: 4

Ingredients:

- 1 Optavia dark chocolate covered cherry shake
- ½ teaspoons baking powder
- 2 tablespoons water

Directions:

1. At 350 degrees F, preheat your oven.
2. Mix cherry shake with water and baking powder in a bowl.
3. Divide this batter on a baking sheet, lined with parchment paper, into 8 small cookies.
4. Bake these cookies 12 minutes in the preheated oven.
5. Serve.

How to serve: Serve the cookies with fresh berries on top.

Optional: Add cherry preserves at the centre of the cookies.

Per Serving:

Calories 118 | Fat 20g | Sodium 192mg | Carbs 23.7g | Fiber 0.9g | Sugar 19g | Protein 5.2g

Stuffed pears with almonds

Preparation Time: 15 minutes.

Cooking Time: 25 minutes.

Servings: 6

Ingredients:

Spices

- 4 pinches cinnamon
- 3 ounces flour
- 3 ounces granulated sugar
- 2 tablespoons soup brown sugar
- 3 ounces almonds, powdered
- 1 ½ ounces frilled almond
- 1 ½ ounces hazelnut
- 3 ½ ounces butter
- 6 pears

Directions:

1. Mix butter with cinnamon, sugars, flour, almonds, hazelnut in a food processor.
2. Core the pears and divide the nuts mixture into these pears.
3. Place the stuffed pears on a baking sheet.
4. Bake these pears for 25 minutes in the oven at 300 degrees F.
5. Serve once cooled.

How to serve: Serve the pears with a scoop of vanilla cream on top.

Optional: Add chopped pecans to the filling as well.

Per Serving:

Calories 248 | Fat 16g |Sodium 95mg | Carbs 38.4g | Fiber 0.3g | Sugar 10g | Protein 14.1g

Peanut Butter Cups

Preparation Time: 15 minutes.

Cooking Time: 12 minutes.

Servings: 4

Ingredients:

- 1/4 cup creamy peanut butter
- 5 ounces chocolate
- Cacao Nibs, Sea Salt

Directions:

1. Melt chocolate with peanut butter in a bowl by heating it in the microwave.
2. Mix well and divide this mixture into 12 mini muffin cups.
3. Cover and refrigerate for 1 hour.
4. Serve.

How to serve: Serve the cups with chocolate or apple sauce.

Optional: Dip the bites in white chocolate syrup.

Per Serving:

Calories 117 | Fat 12g | Sodium 79mg | Carbs 24.8g | Fiber 1.1g | Sugar 18g | Protein 5g

Medifast Rolls

Preparation Time: 15 minutes.

Cooking Time: 35 minutes.

Servings: 4

Ingredients:

- 3 eggs, separated
- 3 tablespoons cream cheese
- Pinch cream of tartar
- 1 packet Splenda

Directions:

1. At 350 degrees F, preheat your oven.
2. Beat separated egg whites with cream of tartar in a bowl until fluffy.
3. Blend yolks with Splenda and cream cheese in a bowl until pale.
4. Fold in egg whites and mix gently.
5. Layer a baking sheet with parchment paper.
6. Divide the batter onto the baking sheet into cookie rounds.
7. Bake these rolls for 35 minutes in the oven at 350 degrees F.
8. Serve once cooled.

How to serve: Serve the rolls with creamy frosting on top.

Optional: Add chopped pecans or walnuts to the batter.

Per Serving:

Calories 195 | Fat 3g | Sodium 355mg | Carbs 20g | Fiber 1g | Sugar 25g | Protein 1g

Apple Crisp

Preparation Time: 15 minutes.

Cooking Time: 40 minutes.

Servings: 4

Ingredients:

- 4 cups apples, peeled and sliced
- 1 tablespoon coconut oil, melted
- 1/2 teaspoon cinnamon
- 1/4 teaspoon ground ginger

Crisp Topping

- ½ teaspoon cinnamon
- ¼ teaspoon ginger
- ¼ teaspoon nutmeg
- 1 cup old fashioned oats
- 1/3 cup pecans chopped
- 2 tablespoons coconut oil
- 1 tablespoon maple syrup

Directions:

1. At 350 degrees F, preheat your oven. Grease an 8x8 inch baking dish.
2. Toss apples with coconut oil, ginger and cinnamon in a bowl.
3. Spread the apples in the baking dish.
4. Mix all the crisp topping in a bowl and drizzle over the apples.

5. Cover this baking dish with aluminium foil and bake for 20 minutes at 350 degrees F.
6. Uncover the hot dish and bake for another 20 minutes.
7. Serve.

How to serve: Serve the apple crisp with chopped nuts on top.

Optional: Add dried raisins to the apple crisp.

Per Serving:

Calories 203 | Fat 8.9g |Sodium 340mg | Carbs 24.7g | Fiber 1.2g | Sugar 11.3g | Protein 5.3g

Cherry Dessert

Preparation Time: 15 minutes.

Cooking Time: 0 minutes.

Servings: 4

Ingredients:

- 2 cups lite whipped topping, thawed
- 1 (8-ounce) package cream cheese, softened
- 1 package sugar-free cherry gelatin
- 1/2 cup boiling water

Directions:

1. Beat cream with cream cheese in a bowl until smooth.
2. Mix gelatin mix with boiling water in a bowl.
3. Add this prepared gelatin mixture to the cream cheese mixture.
4. Mix well and spread this mixture into a pie pan.
5. Cover and refrigerate the cream cheese for 2 hours.
6. Serve.

How to serve: Serve the cherry dessert with fresh berries on top.

Optional: Add vanilla extracts to the dessert.

Per Serving:

Calories 153 | Fat 1g | Sodium 8mg | Carbs 66g | Fiber 0.8g | Sugar 56g | Protein 1g

Vanilla Pudding

Preparation Time: 15 minutes.
Cooking Time: 8 minutes.
Servings: 4
Ingredients:

- 2 cups of milk
- 1/4 teaspoon salt
- 1/2 cup milk
- 3 tablespoons cornstarch
- 3/4 teaspoons pure vanilla extract
- 1/8 teaspoons stevia
- 2 teaspoons buttery spread

Directions:

1. Warm 2 cup milk in a saucepan.
2. Mix cornstarch with ½ cup milk in a bowl and pour into the saucepan.
3. Cook this milk mixture for 3 minutes until it thickens,
4. Stir in remaining ingredients, then mix well.
5. Allow this pudding to cool and serve.

How to serve: Serve the pudding with chocolate syrup or berries on top.

Optional: Add crushed walnuts or pecans to the custard.

Per Serving:

Calories 198 | Fat 14g |Sodium 272mg | Carbs 34g | Fiber 1g | Sugar 9.3g | Protein 1.3g

Banana Cookies

Preparation Time: 10 minutes.
Cooking Time: 15 minutes.
Servings: 4
Ingredients:

- 2 ripe bananas
- 1/3 cup almond milk
- 1 cup all-purpose flour
- 1/2 teaspoon baking powder

Directions:

1. At 350 degrees F, preheat your oven.
2. Mash bananas with almond milk in a mixing bowl.
3. Stir in baking powder and flour, then mix well.
4. Divide the batter into 13 cookies using a scoop onto a baking sheet with parchment paper.
5. Bake these cookies for 15 minutes in the oven.
6. Allow the cookies to cool.
7. Serve.

How to serve: Serve the cookies with chocolate sauce.
Optional: Roll the cookies in crushed nuts or coconut flakes before cooking.
Per Serving:
Calories 159 | Fat 3g | Sodium 277mg | Carbs 21g | Fiber 1g | Sugar 9g | Protein 2g

Sweet Potato Cheesecake

Preparation Time: 10 minutes.
Cooking Time: 15 minutes.
Servings: 6
Ingredients:

- 1 egg, whole
- ¼ cup yogurt cheese
- 1/2 cup coconut milk
- 1/8 teaspoons pumpkin pie spice
- ½ teaspoons vanilla
- 1 tablespoon maple syrup
- 2 package optavia honey sweet potatoes
- ½ teaspoons sweet leaf stevia powdered

To garnish:

- 15 almonds, chopped

Directions:

1. Blend honey sweet potato fueling with the rest of the ingredients in a bowl.
2. Divide this mixture into 6 muffin cups and drizzle almond on top.
3. Bake for 15 in the oven at 350 degrees F.
4. Serve.

How to serve: Serve the cakes with cream frosting on top.
Optional: Add chocolate chips or a teaspoon of crushed nuts to the batter for the change of flavor.

Per Serving:

Calories 245 | Fat 14g | Sodium 122mg | Carbs 23.3g | Fiber 1.2g | Sugar 12g | Protein 4.3g

Cauliflower Breakfast Casserole

Preparation Time: 10 minutes.

Cooking Time: 55 minutes.

Servings: 8

Ingredients:

- 8 ounces turkey sausage, cooked
- ¼ cup onion, chopped
- 2 cups cauliflower florets
- ½ teaspoon Jalapeno Seasoning
- ¼ teaspoon salt
- ¼ teaspoon black pepper
- 6 turkey bacon slices, cooked and chopped
- 2 cups Mexican cheese, shredded
- 8 large eggs
- 16 ounces egg whites
- ¼ cup almond milk

Directions:

1. At 350 degrees F, preheat your oven.
2. Grease a baking dish with cooking spray.
3. Saute turkey sausage in a skillet until golden brown.
4. Saute onions and cauliflower in a same skillet until golden.
5. Stir in black pepper, salt, jalapeno seasoning then mix well.

6. Sread the cauliflower mixture in the prepared baking dish.
7. Top this mixture with cheese and bacon.
8. Beat egg whites with eggs and almond milk in a bowl.
9. Pour this mixture over the turkey mixture.
10. Bake for 45 minutes in the oven.
11. Garnish with green onions.
12. Serve warm.

How to serve: Enjoy this breakfast casserole with a refreshing smoothie.

Optional: Add some chopped or shredded zucchini to the casserole.

Per Serving:
Calories 244 | Fat 7.9g |Sodium 704mg | Carbs 19g | Fiber 2g | Sugar 14g | Protein 14g

Quinoa Pudding

Preparation Time: 10 minutes.

Cooking Time: 25 minutes.

Servings: 4

Ingredients:

- 1 cup quinoa
- 4 cups coconut milk
- 1/3 cup maple syrup
- 1 ½ teaspoons vanilla extract
- 1 teaspoon cinnamon
- 1/4 teaspoon salt

Directions:

1. Mix quinoa, milk, maple, vanilla, cinnamon and salt in a saucepan.
2. Boil this mixture, reduce the heat and cook for 25 minutes.
3. Garnish with your favorite toppings.
4. Serve warm.

How to serve: Serve this pudding with toasted bread slices.

Optional: Add chopped berries and nuts to the pudding.

Per Serving:

Calories 214 | Fat 5.1g |Sodium 231mg | Carbs 31g | Fiber 5g | Sugar 2.1g | Protein 7g

Cranberry Sweet Potato Muffins

Preparation Time: 15 minutes.

Cooking Time: 20 minutes.

Servings: 4

Ingredients:

- 2 tablespoons butter, melted
- 1/4 cup brown sugar
- 1 egg
- 1 teaspoon vanilla
- 1/4 cup skim milk
- 1/2 cup curd cottage cheese
- 1/2 cup cooked sweet potato, mashed
- 3/4 cup white whole wheat flour
- 1 teaspoon baking powder
- 1 cup fresh cranberries

Directions:

1. Mix all the ingredients for batter in a bowl until smooth.
2. Stir in cranberries then divide the batter into muffin cups.
3. Bake for 20 minutes at 350 degrees F.
4. Allow the cranberries to cool then serve.

How to serve: Enjoy these muffins with a refreshing smoothie.

Optional: Add some riasins to the muffins.

Per Serving:

Calories 225 | Fat 9g | Sodium 118mg | Carbs 35.4g | Fiber 2.9g | Sugar 15g | Protein 6.5g

Quinoa Bars

Preparation Time: 15 minutes.
Cooking Time: 20 minutes.
Servings: 6
Ingredients:

- 1 cup whole wheat flour
- 1 ½ cup cooked quinoa
- 2 cup oats
- 1/2 cup nuts, chopped
- 1 teaspoon cinnamon
- 1 teaspoon baking soda
- 2 tablespoons chia seeds
- 2/3 cup peanut butter
- 1/2 cup honey
- 2 eggs
- 2/3 cup applesauce
- 1teaspoons vanilla
- 1/2 teaspoon salt
- 1/3 cup craisins
- 1/3 cup chocolate chips

Directions:

1. Mix quinoa with honey, peanut butter, eggs, vanilla, applesauce in a small bowl.
2. Stir in rest of the ingredients then mix well.

3. Spread this mixture in a 9x13 greased baking dish.
4. Bake for 20 minutes at 375 degrees F then cut into bars.
5. Serve.

How to serve: Enjoy these bars with a strawberry smoothie.

Optional: Add some goji berries to the bars.

Per Serving:
Calories 163 | Fat 2.5g |Sodium 15.6mg | Carbs 49.5g | Fiber 7.6g | Sugar 28g | Protein 3.5g

Buckwheat Crepes

Preparation Time: 15 minutes.

Cooking Time: 10 minutes.

Servings: 4

Ingredients:

- 2/3 cup buckwheat flour
- 1/3 cup whole wheat flour
- 2 eggs
- 1 ¼ cup skim milk
- 1 tablespoon honey
- Fruit and Greek yogurt, for filling

Directions:

1. Mix flours with eggs, milk, and honey in a bowl until smooth.
2. Set a nonstick skillet over medium heat.
3. Add a ¼ cup batter into the skillet, spread it evenly then cook for 2 minutes per side.
4. Transfer the crepe to a plate and then cook the remaining batter in the same way.
5. Garnish with fruits and yogurt.
6. Serve.

How to serve: Enjoy these crepes with a blueberry smoothie.

Optional: Add some blueberries to the crepes filling.

Per Serving:

Calories 112 | Fat 25g |Sodium 132mg | Carbs 44g | Fiber 3.9g | Sugar 3g | Protein 8.9g

Oatmeal Pancakes

Preparation Time: 10 minutes.

Cooking Time: 10 minutes.

Servings: 6

Ingredients:

- 2/3 cup Greek Yogurt
- 3 tablespoons skim milk
- 1 tablespoon applesauce
- 1 egg
- 1/2 cup white whole wheat flour
- 3/4 cup oats, crushed
- 1 teaspoon baking powder
- 1/2 teaspoon baking soda
- 1 tablespoon ground flaxseed
- 1 teaspoon cinnamon

Directions:

1. Mix flours and rest of the ingredients in a bowl until smooth.
2. Set a hot griddle over medium heat.
3. Pour a ladle of battter over the griddle and cook the pancake for 2 mintues per side.
4. Transfer to a plate and cook remaining pancakes in the same manner.
5. Serve warm.

How to serve: Enjoy these pancakes with a spinach smoothie.

Optional: Add chopped nuts to the batter.

Per Serving:

Calories 190 | Fat 15g | Sodium 595mg | Carbs 11g | Fiber 3g | Sugar 12g | Protein 9g

Blueberry Muffins

Preparation Time: 15 minutes.

Cooking Time: 30 minutes.

Servings: 4

Ingredients:

- 2 tablespoons butter, melted
- 1 cup fresh blueberries
- 1/4 cup sugar
- 1 egg
- 1 teaspoon vanilla
- 1/4 cup skim milk
- 1/2 cup curd cottage cheese
- 1/2 cup cooked sweet potato, mashed
- 3/4 cup whole wheat flour
- 1 teaspoon baking powder

Directions:

1. Mix sweet potato mash with all the ingredients except cranberries in a bowl until smooth.
2. Fold in blueberries then mix evenly.
3. Divide the batter into the muffin tray and bake for 30 minutes at 350 degrees F.
4. Serve.

How to serve: Enjoy these muffins with a strawberry smoothie.

Optional: Add raisins to the muffin batter.

Per Serving:
Calories 197 | Fat 15g | Sodium 202mg | Carbs 58.5g | Fiber 4g | Sugar 1g | Protein 7.3g

Berry Quinoa

Preparation Time: 10 minutes.

Cooking Time: 20 minutes.

Servings: 4

Ingredients:

- ¼ cup quinoa, rinsed
- 1/2 cup almond milk
- 1/2 cup berries
- 1 dash cinnamon
- 1/2 teaspoon vanilla

Toppings

- Nuts
- Fruit
- Chocolate chips
- Nut butter
- Agave/honey

Directions:

1. Mix quinoa with milk, vanilla, cinnamon and berries in a saucepan.
2. Cook to a boil, reduce its heat and cook for 20 minutes until liquid is absorved.
3. Garnish with desired toppings.
4. Serve.

How to serve: Enjoy this quinoa with a cranberry muffin.

Optional: Add roasted nuts to the quinoa.

Per Serving:

Calories 163 | Fat 6.5g |Sodium 548mg | Carbs 3.4g | Fiber 2g | Sugar 1g | Protein 2g

Celery Salad

Preparation Time: 5 minutes.

Cooking Time: 0 minutes.

Servings: 2

Ingredients:

- 1 cup celery, chopped
- 1 tablespoon mint, chopped
- 1 teaspoon lemon juice
- 1 teaspoon olive oil

Directions:

1. Mix celery with mint, lemon juice and olive oil in a salad bowl.
2. Serve.

How to serve: Serve this salad with grilled shrimp.

Optional: Drizzle dried herbs and cumin on top.

Per Serving:

Calories 148 | Fat 22g |Sodium 350mg | Carbs 32.2g | Fiber 0.7g | Sugar 1g | Protein 4.3g

Taco Salad

-Preparation Time: 5 minutes.

Cooking Time: 0 minutes.

Servings: 2

Ingredients:

- 5 ounces ground turkey
- 1 tablespoon taco seasoning
- 2 tablespoons salsa
- 1 cup romaine lettuce
- 1 cup iceberg lettuce
- 1/2 cup diced tomatoes
- 1 tablespoon water

Directions:

1. Saute turkey with taco seasoning in a skillet until golden brown.
2. Transfer to a salad bowl and stir in salsa, lettuces, tomatoes and water.
3. Mix well and serve.

How to serve: Serve this salad with grilled chicken.

Optional: Drizzle black pepper ground on top before serving.

Per Serving:

Calories 345 | Fat 9g | Sodium 48mg | Carbs 14g | Fiber 1g | Sugar 2g | Protein 20g

Yogurt Trail Mix Bars

Preparation Time: 15 minutes.

Cooking Time: 0 minutes.

Servings: 4

Ingredients:

- 2 cups Greek yogurt
- 1 ½ cups fruit
- 1/2 cup almonds, chopped
- 3/4 cup granola
- 1/4 cup chocolate chips

Directions:

1. Mix yogurt with fruit, almonds, granola and chocolate chips in a bowl.
2. Spread this mixture in a shallow tray and freeze for 1 hour.
3. Cut the mixture into bars.
4. Serve.

How to serve: Serve these bars with a berry compote.

Optional: Pour melted chocolates on top and then slice to serve.

Per Serving:

Calories 204 | Fat 3g | Sodium 216mg | Carbs 17g | Fiber 3g | Sugar 4g | Protein 11g

Curried Tuna Salad

Preparation Time: 15 minutes.

Cooking Time: 0 minutes.

Servings: 2

Ingredients:

- 2 cans of tuna, drained
- ¼ cup hummus
- ¼ cup avocado, smashed
- ½ cup apple, chopped
- ¼ cup onion, diced
- 1 tablespoon lemon juice
- 2 teaspoons curry powder
- 1/2 teaspoon dry mustard powder

Directions:

1. Mix tuna with rest of the ingredients in a salad bowl.
2. Serve fresh.

How to serve: Serve this salad with grilled shrimp.

Optional: Drizzle shredded coconut on top before serving.

Per Serving:

Calories 280 | Fat 9g |Sodium 318mg | Carbs 19g | Fiber 5g | Sugar 3g | Protein 17g

Tuna Quinoa Cakes

Preparation Time: 15 minutes.
Cooking Time: 20 minutes.
Servings: 4
Ingredients:

- 1/2 cup cooked sweet potato, mashed
- 2 cans tuna, drained
- 3/4 cup cooked quinoa
- 1/4 cup green onion, chopped
- 2 garlic cloves, minced
- 1 tablespoon lemon juice
- 1 egg
- 1/4 cup plain yogurt
- 1 tablespoon mustard
- 1/2 teaspoon cayenne pepper
- 1 teaspoon paprika
- 1/2 cup breadcrumbs

Directions:

1. In a small bowl, combine the tuna and sweet potato and mix well.
2. Add remaining ingredients and stir until well combined.
3. Make 6 patties out of this mixture.
4. Place the patties in a greased baking sheet and bake for 20 minutes at 400 degrees F.

5. Flip the patties once cooked half way through.
6. Serve warm.

How to serve: Serve the cakes with cream cheese dip on the side.

Optional: Add shredded parmesan before cooking.

Per Serving:

Calories 273 | Fat 8g |Sodium 146mg | Carbs 18g | Fiber 5g | Sugar 1g | Protein 7g

Taco Cups

Preparation Time: 15 minutes.

Cooking Time: 25 minutes.

Servings: 4

Ingredients:

- 2 Sargento cheese slices
- 4 ounces lean ground beef
- 1 teaspoon taco seasoning

Toppings:

- Lettuce and tomatoes
- 1 tablespoon sour cream

Directions:

1. At 375 degrees F, preheat your oven.
2. Sauté beef in a skillet for 5 minutes.
3. Stir in taco seasoning then mix well.
4. Layer a baking sheet with wax paper.
5. Place cheese slices in the baking sheet and bake for 7 minutes in the oven.
6. Allow the cheese to cool and then place each cheese round in the muffin tray.
7. Press the cheese into cups and divide the beef into these cups.
8. Garnish with desired toppings.
9. Serve warm.

How to serve: Serve the cups with guacamole.

Optional: Add shredded cheese to the filling.

Per Serving:

Calories 240 | Fat 25g |Sodium 244mg | Carbs 16g | Fiber 1g | Sugar 1g | Protein 27g

Caprese Spaghetti Squash Nests

Preparation Time: 15 minutes.

Cooking Time: 1 hr 35 minutes.

Servings: 4

Ingredients:

For the Nests:

- 1 medium spaghetti squash
- 1/4 teaspoon salt
- 1/4 teaspoon black pepper
- 1/4 teaspoon garlic powder
- 3 tablespoons egg whites

Filling:

- 1 cup cherry tomatoes
- 1/4 teaspoon salt
- 1/4 teaspoon black pepper
- 4 ounces mozzarella cheese, shredded
- 1/4 cup basil, chopped

Directions:

1. At 375 degrees F, preheat your oven.
2. Cut the spaghetti squash in half and place in the baking sheet.
3. Bake the squash for 45 minutes in the oven.
4. Scrape the squash with a fork and divide the shreds in the muffin tray.

5. Beat egg whites with garlic powder, black pepper and salt.
6. Divide this liquid mixture into the muffin cups, make a nest at the center of each and bake for 20 minutes.
7. Spread tomatoes in a baking sheet and bake for 20 minutes in the oven.
8. Divide the roasted tomaotes in the spaghetti squash and top them with cheese and rest of the ingredients.
9. Bake for 10 minutes in the oven.
10. Serve warm.

How to serve: Serve the nests with spinach or cream cheese dip.

Optional: Add shredded parmesan on top.

Per Serving:

Calories 282 | Fat 4g |Sodium 232mg | Carbs 7g | Fiber 1g | Sugar 0g | Protein 14g

Fire Cracker Shrimp

Preparation Time: 15 minutes.
Cooking Time: 6 minutes.
Servings: 4
Ingredients:

- 11 ounces raw shrimp, peeled
- 2 tablespoons Apricot Preserves
- 1 teaspoon lite soy sauce
- ½ teaspoon sriracha sauce
- 1 teaspoon sesame oil

Directions:

1. Place apricot in a small bowl and heat for 20 seconds in the microwave.
2. Mix oil, sriracha sauce, soy sauce and apricot mixture in a bowl.
3. Thread the shrimp on the wooden skewers and brush them with apricot mixture.
4. Grill these skewers for 3 minutes per side.
5. Serve warm.

How to serve: Serve the shrimp with zucchini fries.
Optional: Add crumbled cheese on top.
Per Serving:
Calories 229 | Fat 5g | Sodium 510mg | Carbs 37g | Fiber 5g | Sugar 4g | Protein 21g

Crispy Zucchini Chips

Preparation Time: 15 minutes.

Cooking Time: 4 hrs.

Servings: 4

Ingredients:

- 1 ½ cups zucchini
- 1 teaspoon olive oil
- 1/8 teaspoons salt

Directions:

1. At 200 degrees F, preheat your oven.
2. Layer a baking sheet with wax paper and grease with cooking spray.
3. Spread the zucchini slices in the baking sheet and bake for 4 hours.
4. Flip the zucchinin once cooked half way through.
5. Serve warm.

How to serve: Serve the chips with tomato sauce.

Optional: Drizzle black pepper on top before serving.

Per Serving:

Calories 101 | Fat 7g | Sodium 269mg | Carbs 5g | Fiber 4g | Sugar 12g | Protein 1g

Baked Kale Chips

Preparation Time: 15 minutes.

Cooking Time: 15 minutes.

Servings: 4

Ingredients:

- 4 ½ cups kale
- 1 tablespoon olive oil
- 1/4 teaspoon salt

Directions:

1. At 450-degree F, preheat your oven.
2. Layer a baking sheet with parchment paper.
3. Toss the kale leaves with salt, and olive oil in the baking sheet.
4. Spread them evenly then bake for 15 minutes in the oven.
5. Serve.

How to serve: Serve these chips with chilli garlic sauce.

Optional: Add some paprika or red pepper flakes to the topping.

Per Serving:

Calories 118 | Fat 11g | Sodium 110mg | Carbs 4g | Fiber 5g | Sugar 3g | Protein 1g

Chia Seed Pudding

Preparation Time: 15 minutes.

Cooking Time: 0 minute.

Servings: 2

Ingredients:

- 2 cups almond milk
- 1/2 cup chia seeds
- 1/4 cup almond butter
- 1/4 cup cocoa powder unsweetened
- 4 dates large, pitted and chopped
- 1 teaspoon pure vanilla extract

Directions:

1. Blend all the pudding ingredients in a bowl.
2. Cover and refrigerate this pudding for 4 hours.
3. Serve.

How to serve: Serve the pudding with goji berries on top.

Optional: Add white chocolate syrup on top.

Per Serving:

Calories 361 | Fat 10g | Sodium 218mg | Carbs 56g | Fiber 10g | Sugar 30g | Protein 4g

Grilled Buffalo Shrimp

Preparation Time: 15 minutes.

Cooking Time: 8 minutes.

Servings: 4

Ingredients:

- 11 ounce raw shrimp, peeled
- 1/4 cup Frank's Hot Sauce
- 1 tablespoon butter

Directions:

1. Mix butter with hot sauce in a bowl.
2. Thread the shrimp on the skewers and brush them with butter mixture.
3. Grill these skewers for 2 minutes per side while basting with butter sauce.
4. Serve warm.

How to serve: Serve the shrimps with tomato ketchup.

Optional: Coat the shrimp in breadcrumbs before cooking.

Per Serving:

Calories 275 | Fat 16g | Sodium 255mg | Carbs 1g | Fiber 1.2g | Sugar 5g | Protein 19g

Strawberry Ice Cream

Preparation Time: 10 minutes.

Cooking Time: 0 minutes.

Servings: 6

Ingredients:

- 16 ounce strawberries, frozen
- 3/4 cup Greek yogurt plain
- 2 tablespoons balsamic vinegar
- 2 tablespoons honey

Directions:

1. Blend all the ingredients for ice cream in a blender until smooth.
2. Divide the mixture in the ice-cream molds.
3. Freeze the ice cream for 4 hours.
4. Serve.

How to serve: Serve the ice cream with fresh berries on top.

Optional: Add strawberry preserves on top of the ice cream.

Per Serving:

Calories 118 | Fat 20g | Sodium 192mg | Carbs 23.7g | Fiber 0.9g | Sugar 19g | Protein 5.2g

Strawberry Yogurt

Preparation Time: 5 minutes.

Cooking Time: 0 minutes.

Servings: 2

Ingredients:

Spices

- 1 cup Greek yogurt plain
- 3/4 cup strawberry fruit spread

Directions:

1. Blend yogurt with strawberries in a blender.
2. Serve.

How to serve: Serve the yogurt with berries on top.

Optional: Add chopped pecans to the yogurt as well.

Per Serving:

Calories 248 | Fat 16g | Sodium 95mg | Carbs 38.4g | Fiber 0.3g | Sugar 10g | Protein 14.1g

Banana Pops

Preparation Time: 15 minutes.
Cooking Time: 0 minutes.
Servings: 2
Ingredients:

- 3 bananas
- 3 tablespoons cacao powder raw
- 2 liquid stevia drops
- 3 ounces water
- 1/4 cup cacao nibs raw
- 1/4 cup goji berries raw

Directions:

1. Insert a stick into each banana.
2. Place these bananas in the freezer for 30 minutes.
3. Mash the remaining banana with stevia, water and cacao powder in a bowl.
4. Dip the bananas on the stick in the cacao mmixture.
5. Coat them with cacao nibs and gji berries.
6. Serve.

How to serve: Serve the pops with chocolate or apple sauce.

Optional: Dip the bananas in white chocolate syrup.

Per Serving:

Calories 117 | Fat 12g | Sodium 79mg | Carbs 24.8g | Fiber 1.1g | Sugar 18g | Protein 5g

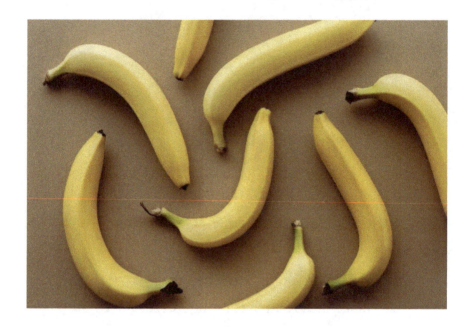

Strawberry Cheesecake

Preparation Time: 15 minutes.

Cooking Time: 0 minutes.

Servings: 6

Ingredients:

- 1/2 cup cream cheese
- 2 tablespoons coconut palm sugar
- 1/2 cup Greek yogurt
- 2 teaspoons lemon juice, squeezed
- 1/4 cup strawberry preserves
- 1 cup strawberries diced
- 1/3 cup almonds whole
- 4 dates

Directions:

1. Beat cream cheese with lemon juice, yogurt, and sugar in a blender for 3 minutes.
2. Mix strawberries with preserves in a small bowl.
3. Grind the almonds with dates in a food processor.
4. Divide the almond mixture in a muffin tray and press it.
5. Add cheesecake batter on top and divide the strawberry mixture on top.
6. Refirgerate these mini cheese cakes for 1 hour.
7. Serve.

How to serve: Serve the cheese cakes with creamy frosting on top.

Optional: Add chopped pecans or walnuts to the batter.

Per Serving:

Calories 195 | Fat 3g |Sodium 355mg | Carbs 20g | Fiber 1g | Sugar 25g | Protein 1g

Coffee Cake Muffins

Preparation Time: 15 minutes.

Cooking Time: 15 minutes.

Servings: 4

Ingredients:

- 1 packet medifast cappuccino
- 1 packet medifast chocolate chip pancakes
- 1 packet of stevia
- 1 tablespoon egg, beaten
- 1/4 teaspoon baking powder
- 1/4 cup water

Directions:

1. Mix cappuccino fueling and rest of the ingredients in a bowl until smooth.
2. Divide the mixture into the muffin tray.
3. Bake the muffins for 15 minutes in the oven at 350 degrees F.
4. Allow the muffins to cool and serve.

How to serve: Serve the muffins with chopped nuts on top.

Optional: Add dried raisins to the muffins.

Per Serving:

Calories 203 | Fat 8.9g | Sodium 340mg | Carbs 24.7g | Fiber 1.2g | Sugar 11.3g | Protein 5.3g

Peanut Butter Balls

Preparation Time: 15 minutes.

Cooking Time: 0 minutes.

Servings: 4

Ingredients:

- 1 Medifast chocolate pudding
- 1 Medifast chocolate shake
- 4 tablespoons powdered peanut butter
- 2 tablespoons water
- 1/4 cup unsweetened almond milk

Directions:

1. Mix chocolate pudding and all the ingredients in a bowl.
2. Make 8 fudge balls out of this mixture.
3. Place the fudge balls in a baking sheet and refrigerate for 4 hours.
4. Serve.

How to serve: Serve the balls with chopped nuts on top.

Optional: Add vanilla extracts to the dessert.

Per Serving:

Calories 153 | Fat 1g | Sodium 8mg | Carbs 66g | Fiber 0.8g | Sugar 56g | Protein 1g

Brownie in a Tray

Preparation Time: 15 minutes.
Cooking Time: 1 minutes.
Servings: 4
Ingredients:

- 1 Medifast Brownie Mix
- 3 tablespoons water
- 1 wedge cream cheese
- 2 tablespoons Peanut butter powder
- 1 tablespoon water

Directions:

6. Blend brownie mix with 3 tbs water in a shallow bowl.
7. Heat this mixture in the microwave for 1 minutes.
8. Slice the cream cheese slices and place on top of the brownie.
9. Blend peanut butter powder with 1 tablespoon water in a bowl.
10. Pour this mixture over the brownie.
11. Serve.

How to serve: Serve the brownie with chocolate syrup or berries on top.

Optional: Add crushed walnuts or pecans to the brownie.

Per Serving:

Calories 198 | Fat 14g | Sodium 272mg | Carbs 34g | Fiber 1g | Sugar 9.3g | Protein 1.3g

Dark Chocolate Mousse

Preparation Time: 10 minutes.

Cooking Time: 0 minutes.

Servings: 2

Ingredients:

- 2 ripe avocados, peeled and pitted
- ½ cup dark cocoa powder
- 1 tablespoon vanilla extract
- ¼ cup stevia powder
- ¼ cup almond milk
- 1 pinch salt

Directions:

1. Blend all avocados with rest of the ingredients in a blender until smooth.
2. Cover and refrigerate the mousse for 1 hour.
3. Garnish and serve.

How to serve: Serve the mousse with chocolate sauce on top.

Optional: Add crushed nuts or coconut flakes.

Per Serving:

Calories 159 | Fat 3g | Sodium 277mg | Carbs 21g | Fiber 1g | Sugar 9g | Protein 2g

Banana Pudding

Preparation Time: 10 minutes.

Cooking Time: 15 minutes.

Servings: 4

Ingredients:

Cookie layer:

- 2 tablespoons butter softened
- 1 teaspoon vanilla extract
- 1 egg
- 1/2 cup almond flour
- 1 teaspoon baking powder
- 1/4 cup erythritol

Pudding layer:

- 2 cups heavy whipping cream
- 1 cup almond milk
- 2 teaspoons vanilla extract
- 6 egg yolks
- 1/2 cup erythritol
- 1 medium banana, sliced

Whipped cream layer:

- 1/2 cup heavy whipping cream
- 1 teaspoon vanilla extract
- 1/4 cup erythritol
- 1/4 teaspoon xanthan gum

Directions:
1. At 350 degrees F, preheat your oven.
2. Layer a baking sheet with parchment paper.
3. Mix butter with egg and vanilla in a bowl.
4. Stir in baking powder, almond flour and erythritol then mix well.
5. Spread this mixture in an 8x16 inches baking sheet.
6. Bake this batter for 15 minutes until golden brown.
7. Meanwhile, mix all the pudding ingredients in a saucepan and cook until the pudding thickens.
8. Spread the pudding over the baked cookie layer.
9. Beat all the cream layer ingredients in a bowl until fluffy.
10. Spread this mixture over the pudding layer.
11. Cover and refrigerate for 1 hour.
12. Slice and serve.

How to serve: Serve the pudding cups with peanut butter frosting on top.

Optional: Add chocolate chips or a teaspoon of crushed nuts to the batter for the change of flavor.

Per Serving:
Calories 268 | Fat 14g | Sodium 122mg | Carbs 23.3g | Fiber 1.2g | Sugar 12g | Protein 6g

Garlic Chicken with Zoodles

Preparation Time: 15 minutes.

Cooking Time: 28 minutes.

Servings: 4

Ingredients:

- 1 ½ lbs boneless chicken breasts
- 1 tablespoon olive oil
- 1 cup Greek yogurt
- ½ cup chicken broth
- ½ teaspoons garlic powder
- ½ teaspoons Italian seasoning
- ¼ cup parmesan cheese
- 1 cup spinach, chopped
- 6 sun-dried tomatoes slices
- 1 tablespoon garlic, chopped
- 1 ½ cups zucchini, cut into thin noodles

Directions:

1. Pat dry the chicken breasts and rub them with cooking oil, black pepper and salt.
2. Sear the chicken in a skillet for 5 minutes per side until golden brown.
3. Transfer this prepared chicken to a plate and keep it aside.

4. Mix parmesan cheese, Italian seasoning, garlic powder, chicken broth and yogurt in a large skillet.
5. Mix and cook this mixture until it thickens.
6. Stir in sun-dried tomatoes and spinach, then cook for 3 minutes.
7. Toss in zucchini noodles and place the chicken on top.
8. At 350 degrees F, preheat your oven.
9. Bake the chicken and zucchini noodles for 15 minutes.
10. Serve warm.

How to serve: Serve the zoodles with a kale salad on the side.

Optional: Coat the chicken with coconut shreds.

Per Serving:

Calories 414 | Fat 15g | Sodium 587mg | Carbs 8g | Fiber 1g | Sugar 5g | Protein 60g

Chicken Zucchini Boats

Preparation Time: 15 minutes.

Cooking Time: 50 minutes.

Servings: 4

Ingredients:

- 4 zucchinis
- 1 lb. ground chicken
- 1/4 teaspoon salt
- 1/4 teaspoon black pepper
- 2 garlic cloves, minced
- 1 cup pasta sauce
- 1/4 cup parmesan cheese, grated
- 1/2 cup mozzarella cheese, shredded
- Sliced fresh basil for topping

Directions:

1. At 400 degrees F, preheat your oven.
2. Layer a 9x13 inch baking pan with cooking spray.
3. Sauté chicken with black pepper and salt in a skillet for 10 minutes.
4. Add garlic and cook for 1 minute.
5. Stir in pasta sauce and sauté for 3 minutes.
6. Slice each zucchini boat in half, lengthwise and scoop out some flesh from the centre.
7. Divide the chicken into each zucchini half.

8. Place the prepared zucchini boats in the baking dish with cut-side up.
9. Sprinkle parmesan and mozzarella cheese on top.
10. Cover this baking dish with foil and bake for 35 minutes.
11. Sprinkle basil and serve.

How to serve: Serve the zucchini boats with fresh herbs on top and a bowl of steamed rice.

Optional: Add some chopped bell pepper to the filling.

Per Serving:

Calories 332 | Fat 18g |Sodium 611mg | Carbs 13.3g | Fiber 0g | Sugar g4 | Protein 38g

Medifast Chicken Fry

Preparation Time: 15 minutes.

Cooking Time: 10 minutes.

Servings: 4

Ingredients:

- 12 ounces boneless chicken breast
- 1 cup red bell pepper, chopped
- 1 cup green bell pepper, chopped
- 8 ounces broccoli slaw
- 1/2 cup chicken broth
- 2 tablespoons soy sauce
- 1 teaspoon crushed red pepper

Directions:

1. Sauté broccoli slaw and peppers in a pan with chicken broth.
2. Stir in chicken, red pepper and soy sauce.
3. Cook for 10 minutes with occasional stirring.
4. Serve warm.

How to serve: Serve the stir fry with roasted green beans.

Optional: Add some sliced onion and spring onion to the fry.

Per Serving:

Calories 235 | Fat 5g | Sodium 422mg | Carbs 16g | Fiber 0g | Sugar 1g | Protein 25g

Tuscan Chicken

Preparation Time: 15 minutes.

Cooking Time: 23 minutes.

Servings: 4

Ingredients:

- 1 lb. boneless chicken breasts, sliced
- 2 tablespoons butter spread
- 4 cups kale leaves, chopped
- 2 garlic cloves, chopped
- 1 package Knorr rice sides cheddar broccoli
- ¼ cup sun-dried tomatoes, sliced
- Lemon wedges

Directions:

1. Rub the chicken with black pepper and salt.
2. Sear the chicken with 1 tablespoon butter in a skillet for 5 minutes per side.
3. Transfer this prepared chicken to a plate and keep it aside.
4. Sauté garlic and kale with remaining butter in the same skillet over medium-high heat for 3 minutes.
5. Stir in 2 cup water and cheddar broccoli, and tomatoes then cook for 5 minutes with occasional stirring.

6. Return the cooked chicken to the skillet and cook for 5 minutes.
7. Garnish with lemon wedges and pine nuts.
8. Enjoy.

How to serve: Serve the chicken with roasted veggies.

Optional: Replace kale with baby spinach if needed.

Per Serving:

Calories 369 | Fat 14g | Sodium 442mg | Carbs 13.3g | Fiber 0.4g | Sugar 2g | Protein 32.3g

Chicken Taco Soup

Preparation Time: 15 minutes.

Cooking Time: 5 hours.

Servings: 4

Ingredients:

- 2 cups chicken broth
- 1/2 teaspoon cumin
- 2 cups of water
- 1 cup Rotel diced tomatoes
- 1 teaspoon taco seasoning
- 1/4 teaspoon chili powder
- 1 garlic clove, minced
- 14 ounces of raw chicken breasts
- 2 cups cabbage, chopped

Directions:

1. Add all the taco soup ingredients to a crockpot.
2. Cover its lid and cook for 5 hours on low heat.
3. Shred the cooked chicken and return to the soup.
4. Serve warm.

How to serve: Serve the soup with fresh cucumber and couscous salad.

Optional: Add some canned corn kernels to the soup.

Per Serving:

Calories 453 | Fat 2.4g | Sodium 216mg | Carbs 18g | Fiber 2.3g | Sugar 1.2g | Protein 23.2g

Chicken Chili

Preparation Time: 15 minutes.

Cooking Time: 35 minutes.

Servings: 8

Ingredients:

- 8 (6 inches) corn tortillas
- 2 teaspoons vegetable oil
- 1 lb boneless chicken breast, diced
- 1 teaspoon ground cumin
- 1 cup poblano pepper, chopped
- ½ cup onion, chopped
- 1 garlic clove, minced
- 2 (14 ounces) cans of reduced-fat chicken broth
- 2 (15 ounces) cans of pinto beans
- 1 cups salsa Verde
- 2 tablespoons cilantro, minced

Directions:

1. At 400 degrees F, preheat your oven.
2. Cut 4 the tortilla into ½ inch strips and toss them with 1 teaspoon oil.
3. Spread the tortillas on a baking sheet and bake for 12 minutes.
4. Grate the remaining tortillas into pieces and keep them aside.

5. Sauté chicken pieces with 1 teaspoon oil and cumin in a skillet for 5 minutes.
6. Transfer this prepared chicken to a plate and keep it aside.
7. Sauté garlic, onion and poblano peppers in the same skillet for 3 minutes.
8. Add grated tortillas, salsa, beans, broth and chicken, then cook for 15 minutes on a simmer.
9. Garnish with cilantro and baked tortillas.
10. Serve warm.

How to serve: Serve the chili with toasted bread slices.

Optional: Add corn kernels to the chicken chili.

Per Serving:

Calories 354 | Fat 25g | Sodium 412mg | Carbs 22.3g | Fiber 0.2g | Sugar 1g | Protein 28.3g

Lean Green Chicken Soup

Preparation Time: 15 minutes.

Cooking Time: 25 minutes.

Servings: 6

Ingredients:

- 2 quarts chicken broth
- 1 1/2 lbs. boneless chicken breast
- 2 celery stalks, chopped
- 2 cups green beans, chopped
- 1 1/2 cups peas
- 2 cups asparagus, chopped
- 1 cup green onions, diced
- 6 garlic cloves, minced
- 2 cups spinach leaves, chopped
- 1 bunch watercress, chopped
- 1/2 cup parsley leaves, chopped
- 1/3 cup basil leaves, chopped
- 1 teaspoon salt
- 1/2 teaspoon black pepper

Directions:

1. Boil chicken broth in a cooking pot and add chicken breasts.
2. Cook the chicken on a simmer for 15 minutes.
3. Stir in black pepper, salt, garlic, onions, asparagus, peas, green beans and celery.

4. Cook this mixture on a simmer for 10 minutes then remove from the heat.
5. Shred the cooked chicken with a fork.
6. Add basil, parsley, watercress and spinach to the soup.
7. Serve warm.

How to serve: Serve the soup with white rice or sweet potato salad.

Optional: Add some zucchini noodles to the soup.

Per Serving:

Calories 105 | Fat 15g | Sodium 852mg | Carbs 7g | Fiber 2g | Sugar 2g | Protein 15g

Avocado Chicken Salad

Preparation Time: 15 minutes.

Cooking Time: 0 minutes.

Servings: 4

Ingredients:

- 10 ounces cooked chicken breasts, sliced
- 1/2 cup Greek yogurt
- 3 ounces avocado, chopped
- 1/2 teaspoon garlic powder
- 1/4 teaspoon salt
- 1/8 teaspoons black pepper
- 1 tablespoon 1 teaspoon lime juice
- 1/4 cup fresh cilantro, chopped

Directions:

1. Toss chicken with yogurt, avocado and the rest of the ingredients in a salad bowl.
2. Cover and refrigerate for 30 minutes.
3. Serve.

How to serve: Serve the salad with avocado guacamole on top.

Optional: Add boiled peas to the salad.

Per Serving:

Calories 352 | Fat 14g |Sodium 220mg | Carbs 16g | Fiber 0.2g | Sugar 1g | Protein 26g

Chicken Pesto Pasta

Preparation Time: 15 minutes.

Cooking Time: 0 minutes.

Servings: 6

Ingredients:

Kale Pesto

- 3 cups raw kale
- 2 cup fresh basil
- 2 tablespoons olive oil
- 3 tablespoons lemon juice
- 3 garlic cloves
- ¼ teaspoon salt

Pasta Salad

- 2 cups cooked chicken breast, diced
- 6 ounces cooked rotini chickpea pasta
- 1 cup arugula
- 3oz fresh mozzarella, diced

Directions:

1. Blend kale with all the pesto ingredients in a blender until smooth.
2. Cook chicken cubes with pasta, arugula, pesto and mozzarella in a salad bowl.
3. Serve.

How to serve: Serve the pasta with a spinach salad.

Optional: Add canned corns to the pasta.

Per Serving:

Calories 388 | Fat 8g | Sodium 339mg | Carbs 8g | Fiber 1g | Sugar 2g | Protein 13g

Sesame Chicken Fry

Preparation Time: 15 minutes.

Cooking Time: 16 minutes.

Servings: 4

Ingredients:

For the sauce:

- 1/3 cup soy sauce
- ⅓ cup of water
- 3 garlic cloves, minced
- 2 tablespoons coconut sugar
- 1 tablespoon sesame oil
- 1 tablespoon rice vinegar
- 1 tablespoon fresh ginger, grated
- 1 tablespoon sesame seeds
- ½ teaspoon red pepper flakes
- ½ tablespoon arrowroot starch

For the chicken:

- 1/2 tablespoon sesame oil
- 1 lb. lean ground chicken
- ½ teaspoon garlic powder
- Salt and black pepper, to taste

For the veggies:

- ½ tablespoon toasted sesame oil
- 2 large carrots, sliced

- 1 white onion, chopped
- 1 red bell pepper, chopped
- 12 ounces green beans, trimmed

For serving

- ½ cup roasted cashews, chopped
- Scallions
- Extra sesame seeds

Directions:

1. Mix soy sauce, arrowroot starch, red pepper flakes, sesame seeds, ginger, rice vinegar, sesame oil, coconut sugar, garlic, and water in a bowl.
2. Sauté ground chicken with ½ tablespoons sesame oil in a large pot until golden brown.
3. Stir in black pepper, salt and garlic powder.
4. Transfer this meat to a bowl and keep it aside.
5. Sauté onion with carrots and ½ tablespoons sesame oil in the same pan for 4 minutes.
6. Stir in green beans and bell pepper then cook for 8 minutes.
7. Return the chicken to the veggies and cook for 4 minutes.
8. Serve with brown rice or quinoa.
9. Garnish with roasted cashews, scallions and sesame seeds.
10. Enjoy.

How to serve: Serve the chicken fry with steaming white rice.

Optional: Add roasted peanuts on top.

Per Serving:

Calories 301 | Fat 16g |Sodium 189mg | Carbs 32g | Fiber 0.3g | Sugar 0.1g | Protein 28.2g

Teriyaki Chicken Broccoli

Preparation Time: 15 minutes.
Cooking Time: 13 minutes.
Servings: 4
Ingredients:

- 10 ounces chicken strips
- 2 tablespoons teriyaki sauce
- 1 tablespoon fresh garlic, minced
- 1/2 cup yellow onion, diced
- 2 cups broccoli, florets
- 1/4 cup fresh scallions. sliced
- 2 tablespoons water

Directions:

1. Sauté onion and garlic in a non-stick skillet for 5 minutes.
2. Stir in chicken and the rest of the ingredients, then cook for 8 minutes.
3. Serve warm.

How to serve: Serve the chicken broccoli with cauliflower rice.
Optional: Add dried herbs to the mixture for seasoning.
Per Serving:
Calories 231 | Fat 20g | Sodium 941mg | Carbs 30g | Fiber 0.9g | Sugar 1.4g | Protein 14.6g

CPSIA information can be obtained
at www.ICGtesting.com
Printed in the USA
LVHW011239060621
689455LV00002B/141